When The Heart Whispers...

Afzaleen Shaikh

BookLeaf Publishing

India | USA | UK

Made with ❤ on the BookLeaf Publishing Platform
www.bookleafpub.in
www.bookleafpub.com

Dedication

This book is for the dreamers, the believers, and the storytellers—those who find beauty in words, solace in poetry, and courage in their journey.

To my family, whose love and support make this possible, I am forever grateful. To my little sunshine, my dear nephew, your laughter inspires my heart and fills my world with joy.

And to every reader who listens to the whispers of their own heart, may these pages bring you comfort, hope, and a sense of belonging.

This collection is for you.

Preface

Poetry has always been the language of the soul—a bridge between emotions unspoken and moments unseen. *When the Heart Whispers* is a collection of verses that capture the quiet beauty of life, the warmth of love, and the echoes of memories that shape us.

Each poem in this book is a reflection of the emotions we all experience—hope, nostalgia, love, resilience, and the fleeting magic of time. Whether it is the golden glow of fireflies, the embrace of family, the silent strength of solitude, or the courage to chase dreams, every word here carries a whisper of the heart.

This book is a set of 31 poems divided into five sections:
- Dreams & Aspirations (Hope, Strength, and Growth) [Poems 1 to 6]
- Love & Relationships (Family, Friendship, and Bonds) [Poems 7 to 14]
- Nature & Beauty (Magic of the World Around Us) [Poems 15 to 20]
- Reflection & Emotions (Self-Discovery, Solitude, and Inner Strength) [Poems 21 to 25]
- Memories & Farewells (Nostalgia, Goodbyes and Another Chance) [Poems 26 to 31]

This book is not just a collection of poetry; it is an invitation. An invitation to pause, to feel, and to find your own reflections within these pages. If even a single verse resonates with you, brings you comfort, or inspires you, then the whispers of my heart have found their way to yours.

Acknowledgements

No book is ever written alone. It is shaped by the people who touch our lives, the experiences that mold us, and the love that fuels our passion for words.

To my family— your unwavering support, love, and belief in me have given me the courage to put my words into the world. You are the foundation upon which my poetry stands.

To my little nephew— your innocence, laughter, and boundless joy remind me of the pure magic that life holds. You are the heart of many of these poems, and I hope one day, you will find warmth in them too.

To my dear friends— thank you for your encouragement, for being my sounding boards, and for inspiring me through your own stories and dreams.

To every reader who holds this book in their hands— thank you. Your time, your thoughts, and your presence in this poetic journey mean more than words can express. If these pages have spoken to your heart, then my purpose as a writer is fulfilled.

1. Rise and Shine

I'm going to rise,
I'm going to shine,
Reaching high—
The stars are mine.

With wings of faith,
I'll touch the sky,
No turning back—
Just watch me fly.

Through storms and rain,
Through dark and light,
I'll chase my dreams,
I'll win this fight.

No chains can hold,
No fears confine,
With heart so bold,
The world is mine.

The road is long,
But I won't fall,
With strength and hope,
I'll have it all.

2. Soar High

Soar high above the
Uproars of the world,
Open your wings
And let it be unfurled.

Fly high wearing
The eagle's crown,
Let go of all
That weigh you down.

Be astonishing like
The king of birds,
Fly through the barriers
Moving upwards.

Eyes sharp—
Locked on the distant prize,
No storm can shake
No fear can rise.

Soar high in the
Direction of your dream,
Like an eagle who is—
The powerful supreme.

3. A Leap of Faith

Each day that passes by,
Draws me closer, reaching sky.
A silent test of patience,
A challenge to apply.

I may not be there yet,
But I'm not too far away—
With every step I take,
I'm closer than yesterday.

I may soar or I may stumble,
The outcome yet unknown.
I may swim or I may sink,
But what's meant for me is my own.

Change is daunting, yet it's grand,
A path I must await.
All I need is courage now—
To take that leap of faith.

4. Keep Moving Forward

When you face your greatest challenge,
You're closest to your victory.
Look back and see how far you've come—
Keep moving forward, make history.

If you ever feel overwhelmed,
Take a step back and find your smile.
Breathe deep and remember your strength—
Keep moving forward, it's all worthwhile.

Some days will lift you higher,
Some will put you to the test.
Stay positive, count your blessings—
Keep moving forward, give your best.

Small steps in the right direction
Are better than leaps gone wrong.
The road ahead may feel lonely—
Keep moving forward, stay strong.

Don't fear progress that feels too slow,
Only fear standing still.
Be adaptable, trust in yourself—
Keep moving forward, refine your skill.

When life pulls you back with struggles,
Know it's setting you up for something great.
An arrow can only be launched by pulling back—
Keep moving forward, believe in fate.

5. Patience

Don't give up—you're being tested,
Through each trial, you are perfected.
Patience is among your greatest treasures,
A virtue that time has manifested.

You may face the toughest trials,
Doubting your strength and potential.
But trust in patience—don't complain,
For growth is truly essential.

Some days, you may feel lost and blue,
Or weighed down by abandonment.
Yet patience, your silent guide,
Leads you toward enlightenment.

Patience is not just standing still—
It's action in disguise.
It spares you from a hundred regrets,
And helps you to rise.

In time, you'll reach where you belong,
Each step with steady grace.
For those who walk the path of patience,
Will always win the race.

6. All You Need to Do Is "Wait"

When darkness engulfs you,
And the path is out of sight,
All you need to do is wait—
Soon, the sun will shine its light.

When thoughts surround you,
After you've spoken your heart,
All you need to do is wait—
Let them settle, play their part.

When you're left in suspense,
Awaiting what's to come,
All you need to do is wait—
Find some joy and hum a song.

When doubt whispers loudly,
And patience starts to wane,
All you need to do is wait—
Sunshine follows rain.

7. Blessings from the Brightest Star

For you, dear father, strong and true,
A guiding light in all I do.
You stood so tall, so firm, so strong,
A pillar that held me all along.

Through every storm, through every tide,
Your love and strength stood by my side.
You gave your all, asked for no prize,
A hero in my little eyes.

Through fleeting days, though time was few,
Each moment spent was gold with you.
The laughter, lessons, love you gave,
Are treasures that I'll always save.

Now you shine beyond the skies,
The brightest star before my eyes.
Your blessings fall like drops of light,
Guiding me through darkest nights.

8. My Superhero

Do superheroes exist?
The answer remains unknown,
Yet I feel a magic force,
A shield I call my own.

My protector is my Mother,
My strength, my steady guide,
Greater than any superhero,
With love that won't subside.

Through joy and pain, through rise and fall,
In triumph and defeat,
She holds me close and lifts me up—
My safe haven at her feet.

For all the love and light she gives,
I am grateful to the creator
Do Superheroes exist?
Yes, I call her Mother...

9. Sisters for Life

At times like-minded,
At times worlds apart,
Sisters are precious,
Connected by the heart.

A different flower
From the same garden,
Brightens up the day
When all seems to darken.

Always there to encourage,
As a friend and a philosopher,
Sharing incessant conversations,
A trustworthy secret-keeper.

Through laughter and tears,
Through sunshine and rain,
A bond unshaken,
In joy and in pain.

No matter the distance,
No matter the strife,
Side by side, forever—
Sisters for life.

10. My Little Sunshine

You are a gift my heart embraced,
A love so deep, forever placed.
Not my son, but still my child,
A love so pure, so free, so wild.

My sweet nephew, my little light,
You make my world warm and bright.
Not just an aunt, I'm so much more,
With you, I've found what I live for.

Your laughter lights my darkest days,
A guiding star in endless maze.
Because of you, I've found my way,
You are my sunshine, come what may.

For you, I dream, for you, I strive,
Your joy, the reason I feel alive.
Through every storm, through every mile,
I'd walk forever—just to see you smile.

No matter how the years go by,
How high you soar, how far you fly,
You'll always have a place with me,
My little sunshine, endlessly.

11. Hold My Hand

Holding your hand,
I feel so safe,
Turning the world
Into a beautiful place.

Hold my hand,
And show me the way—
To live and to love,
To work and to play.

Let me hold your hand,
Together we grow.
I'll walk beside you,
Wherever you go.

With every step,
Through new and unknown,
We'll laugh, we'll learn,
We'll make it our own.

Through every storm,
Through sunshine and rain,
With hands held tight,
We'll rise again.

12. I'll Be By Your Side

I ain't Wonder Woman,
To fight the troubles you face.
I ain't Captain Marvel,
To fly you to outer space.

I can't run with super speed,
To get you where you need to be.
I can't use telekinesis,
To set your worries free.

I have no superpowers,
To chase your pain away.
But I promise to stand beside you,
Through every night and day.

The only strength I hold,
Is in the bond we share.
Through every joy and challenge,
I'll always be right there.

Like the sun that warms the earth,
Or stars that light the sky,
I'll be by your side,
As the days and years go by.

13. You Are The One

You are the one who
Brings a smile when I am down,
You are the one who
Lifts me up when troubles surround.

Like a light of hope and faith,
You have always been near,
An answer to unspoken prayers,
A voice I always hear.

Like moments that happen
At just the right place and time,
That shape our lives forever,
In ways so rare, so prime.

Your heart is pure, your soul so bright,
A story worth being told,
If life were filled with endless books,
I'd still choose yours to hold.

I truly admire the way you are,
With a soul so warm and bright,
I don't wish for stars or the moon,
Just your presence, day and night.

14. Forehead Kiss

A forehead kiss from you
Reminds me that you care,
A simple touch so gentle,
A love beyond compare.

In moments of despair,
Or times of endless stress,
Your warmth is my comfort,
A sign that I am blessed.

Through highs and lows,
Through laughter and tears,
We'll walk this path together,
Through all the coming years.

With you beside me,
I fear nothing at all,
A forehead kiss reminds me,
You'll catch me if I fall.

No words are needed,
No grand display,
A forehead kiss speaks
What hearts cannot say.

15. A Happy Song

Oh! A brand new day is here,
With endless chances drawing near.
I step outside so bold and strong—
My heart sings a happy song.

I peek outside and watch with glee,
Children laughing, wild and free.
Their cheerful tunes drift all day long,
My heart sings a happy song.

I marvel at the world so bright,
Nature's wonders, pure delight.
The flowers bloom, the birds belong,
My heart sings a happy song.

I stroll along the golden shore,
Waves keep crashing evermore.
The breeze is soft, yet wild and strong,
My heart sings a happy song.

The splendid night now paints the sky,
The stars like lanterns glowing high.
They walk beside me all night long,
My heart sings a happy song.

16. Magical Colours

Living in a world of canvas,
With colours spread all around,
In endless variants and shades,
Where magic in hues is found.

Golden tangles of the rising sun,
The deepest blue of the restless sea,
Earthy brown of the fertile soil,
And crimson flames that burn so free.

Emerald leaves that sway in breeze,
Petals blushing in a rosy hue,
A violet dusk that softly fades,
As twilight paints the sky anew.

The silver moon in snowy grace,
Dances across the midnight high,
While shadowed bats take silent flight,
As fluorescent birds wave goodbye.

A rainbow arches after the rain,
A masterpiece upon the sky,
Merging colours, bright and bold,
A fleeting dream that passes by.

17. Fireflies

Peeking out of my window,
To see the stars dancing low.
It's hard to believe my eyes,
As flickering fireflies rise.

Like tiny heavenly magicians,
Earning all my admiration.
Illuminating the midnight aisle,
A sight that makes my heart smile.

Helping stars light up the city,
A glimpse of nature's poetry.
Scattering love with golden gleam,
Drifting softly like a dream.

Whispering tales in glowing streams,
Guiding lost and weary beams.
A fleeting touch of magic bright,
Painting shadows with their light.

So let them dance, let them soar,
A wonder we should all adore.
For in their glow, the night reveals,
The quiet joy the heart conceals.

18. Magical Snowflakes

The first fall of the magical snow,
In the middle of the night so still.
Drifting softly, a hushed hello,
Weaving dreams with winter's chill.

Songs of mountains, whispers of birds,
Pines and junipers gently sway.
Oh! Look around—it's all so new,
As velvety snowlights dance and play.

Each flake a wish, a story untold,
A fleeting touch of sky's embrace.
Melting softly upon my skin,
Like love's warm kiss in winter's grace.

Footprints fade but memories stay,
Etched in silver, pure and bright.
A fleeting spell, a winter's gift,
Wrapped in whispers of frosted light.

The snow unveils its love's embrace,
Draping trees, fields, and frozen lakes.
Let's walk upon this silken white,
In the realm of Magical Snowflakes.

19. The Dancing Jewel

Beneath the sky so vast and bright,
A peacock twirls in golden light.
Its feathers shimmer, green and blue,
Like drops of rain and morning dew.

With every step, a tale it weaves,
A dance of joy among the leaves.
The earth, enchanted, holds its breath,
As beauty sways with graceful depth.

A crown of gold upon its head,
A thousand hues so richly spread.
It lifts its plume, a painted fan,
A masterpieceâ€"not made by man.

And when the clouds begin to weep,
The peacock sings, its voice so deep.
A melody both bold and free,
A call of love, a mystery.

Oh, natureâ€™s gem, so wild, so grand,
A living dream on silent land.
A peacock dances, proud and true,
A burst of life in emerald hue.

20. The Book

I write and scribble all over you,
With pens and pencils, glitters, and glue.
I sketch and color what I feel,
In red and yellow, black and blue.

You offer endless space to start,
A canvas for my creative heart.
A place to shape my writing skills,
To count, to dream, to grow, be smart.

I can keep you simple and neat,
Or fill your pages, bold and sweet.
You always bring the best in me,
And make my world feel whole, complete.

I lose myself in tales you weave,
Yet find myself in what I believe.
You open doors to endless worlds,
A friend that never lets me grieve.

Through every story, word, and rhyme,
You take me far beyond my time.
A world of wonder, vast and true,
Forever old, yet always new.

21. Mirror, Mirror On The Wall

Mirror, mirror on the wall,
Who's the happiest of them all?
Is it the one with wealth untold,
Or the one whose speeches sway the world?

The one with friends in great supply,
Or the one crowned with beauty's prize?
The scholar with the grandest degree,
Or the earner of the highest fee?

"These are but shadows," the mirror sighed,
"Happiness dwells deep inside.
A heart at peace, a soul set free,
Kindness brings true ecstasy."

So now I know where joy must start,
I'll seek it within my own heart.
Mirror, mirror on the wall,
I am the happiest of them all.

22. Solitude

What is solitude?

They say solitude leads to loneliness,
I say it grants true independence.
Beyond the need to seek approval,
It is the soul's best companion—eternal.

They claim it makes one anti-social,
I see it fosters self-approval.
Breaking free from worldly ties,
Revealing truth where wisdom lies.

They fear solitude may bring confinement,
I know it is the start of enlightenment.
A quiet escape to treasures untold,
Where hidden answers start to unfold.

They insist it breeds inner emptiness,
Yet I find in it pure happiness.
Far from the world's chaotic blare,
Wrapped in solitude's gentle care.

They whisper it deepens heartache,
I trust it offers a new daybreak.

It silently heals the soul and mind,
A refuge for the hurt to unwind.

They speak of sorrow, loss, and pain,
But no rainbow forms without the rain.
So I embrace this tranquil gift,
Where solitude lets my spirit lift.

23. Time Machine

What if I had a time machine?
Which way would I choose to go?
Race ahead to glimpse tomorrow,
Or turn back to rewrite the flow?

I may choose to visit the past,
Not to change or make it stay.
But to relive the moments bright,
And feel their warmth along the way.

Frozen smiles and echoes bright,
Fading whispers, soft and true.
A fleeting touch, a vanished laugh,
Imprinted in time like morning dew.

Yet the heart, a clock so wise,
Knows just when to pause or play.
No machine is ever needed,
To dream of times beyond today.

Tuning to the rhythm inside,
I weave my future, thread by thread.
For time is not just lost or found,
But lived in all the words unsaid.

24. Dance

Put on your dancing shoes,
Step onto the floor.
Believe in yourself,
And live a little more.

Dance is poetry,
Set in motion,
A hidden language,
Of pure emotion.

There are no rules,
So move to your own tune.
Fall in love with yourself,
And make the moment opportune.

Let the rhythm guide you,
Let your spirit soar.
Lose yourself in the music,
And dance like never before.

25. Smile

A smile can change the world,
A smile can make you strong.
The world looks a little brighter—
Smile, and nothing will go wrong.

Wake up every day with a smile,
It's the prettiest thing to wear.
A smile is the best therapy,
So spread its warmth everywhere.

Even routine work feels exciting,
When you add to it a little smile.
A smile is a gift that enriches all,
So make it your lasting style.

A smile speaks a universal language,
It helps new friendships start.
So smile today and smile always—
Nothing shakes a smiling heart.

26. An Old Photograph

This evening, while clearing the shelf,
I found an old photograph,
Tucked inside a hidden diary,
Folded gently in half.

No way to relive that moment,
A time that's gone forever,
Yet a passage back to memories,
To cherish now and ever.

An old photograph is all I have,
A fragment of yesterday's embrace,
A glimpse into a time so pure,
When laughter lit up every space.

Should I tuck it beneath my pillow,
Or lock it deep within my heart?
Or keep it safe inside my pocket,
Until fate no longer keeps us apart?

Though colors may fade, and edges may fray,
Its essence will always remain,
A silent whisper from the past,
Calling me back once again.

27. A Walk Under the Moonlight

Side by side,
Holding on tight,
Laughing together, under the moonlight.

No rush, no noise,
Just you and me,
A moment so simple, yet full of glee.

The warmth in your smile,
The joy in your face,
Turns an ordinary night, into a magical place.

Cherishing stories,
From old times anew,
With you by my side, there's nothing to rue.

No riches I seek,
No treasure profound,
For love like this, is the best to be found.

28. Just Once

You'll see your reflection
In the depth of my eyes,
Step a bit closer,
And look just once.

You'll hear your name
In the melody of my heart,
A song of care and warmth,
Just listen once.

You'll never be alone
Amidst the chaos of life,
I'm right beside you,
Just feel it once.

Your name is written
In every chapter I hold,
A story of bond and trust,
Just read it once.

All the kindness within me
Exists only for you,
A truth unshaken,
Just believe it once.

29. I Treasure Those Days

I treasure those days
When everything seemed bright,
Affection spread all around,
Hugs embracing tight.

I cherish those times
Of endless heartfelt talks,
Hand in hand we wandered,
Enjoying leisurely walks.

Waiting for you then
Was a joy, not a test,
Though times have changed,
I hold those moments best.

Though farewells were spoken,
And paths diverged anew,
The bond we shared remains,
A light that guides me through.

30. Adieu

And then came the night
When the moon dimmed its glow,
The breeze fell silent,
As if it, too, feared to know.

Thinking it was just a dream,
With a fragile hope, I slept.
But morning stole my comfort,
For you had already left.

You held me close, you kept me safe,
Your love was always true.
If time were kind, you would have stayed,
For there was more to do.

You said, "I wish I had more time,"
Then why did you fade from view?
I stand here waiting at the door,
Longing for your last adieu.

31. Another Chance

Each day brings a brand-new start,
A moment to learn, to dream, to dance.
No past mistake can hold me back,
Life always gives another chance.

The road ahead is bright and wide,
With endless paths at every glance.
I trust the journey, step by step,
Embracing yet another chance.

I choose to grow, to rise, to shine,
To cherish love at every stance.
With hope and faith, I move ahead,
Grateful for another chance.

The past is gone, the future calls,
With open arms and an eager glance.
I welcome joy, I welcome change,
Knowing I have another chance.

No dream's too big, no goal too far,
No fear can break my firm expanse.
With courage strong and heart so free,
I'll make the most of every chance.